Brands We Know

Nerf

By Sara Green

203931

Bellwether Media • Minneapolis, MN

Jump into the cockpit and take flight with Pilot books. Your journey will take you on high-energy adventures as you learn about all that is wild, weird, fascinating, and fun!

Library of Congress Cataloging-in-Publication Data

Names: Green, Sara, 1964-
Title: NERF / by Sara Green.
Description: Minneapolis, MN : Bellwether Media, Inc., 2016. | Series:
 Pilot: Brands We Know | Includes bibliographical references and index.
Identifiers: LCCN 2015028669 | ISBN 9781626173491 (hardcover : alk.
paper)
Subjects: LCSH: NERF toys--Juvenile literature.
Classification: LCC GV1220.9 .G74 2016 | DDC 790.1/33--dc23
LC record available at http://lccn.loc.gov/2015028669

Printed in the United States of America, North Mankato, MN.

Table of Contents

What Is Nerf?

Six children arm themselves with Nerf blasters for a backyard battle. Soon, foam darts are flying through the air. The children try to outrun them, but the darts travel fast and far. A player gets hit and is out! The other players fire until their **clips** are empty. After reloading, the action begins again!

Nerf is a popular toy **brand** owned by Hasbro, Inc. This company is one of the largest toy makers in the world. Its **headquarters** is in Pawtucket, Rhode Island. Nerf is well known for its brightly colored toy weapons. These shoot foam **ammunition** or squirt water. Nerf also sells **accessories** for its weapons. Nerf balls and other sports equipment are very popular. People can play with these toys indoors and outdoors. Many kids also test their battle skills with Nerf's online games. When people play with Nerf, they are sure to have fun!

By the Numbers

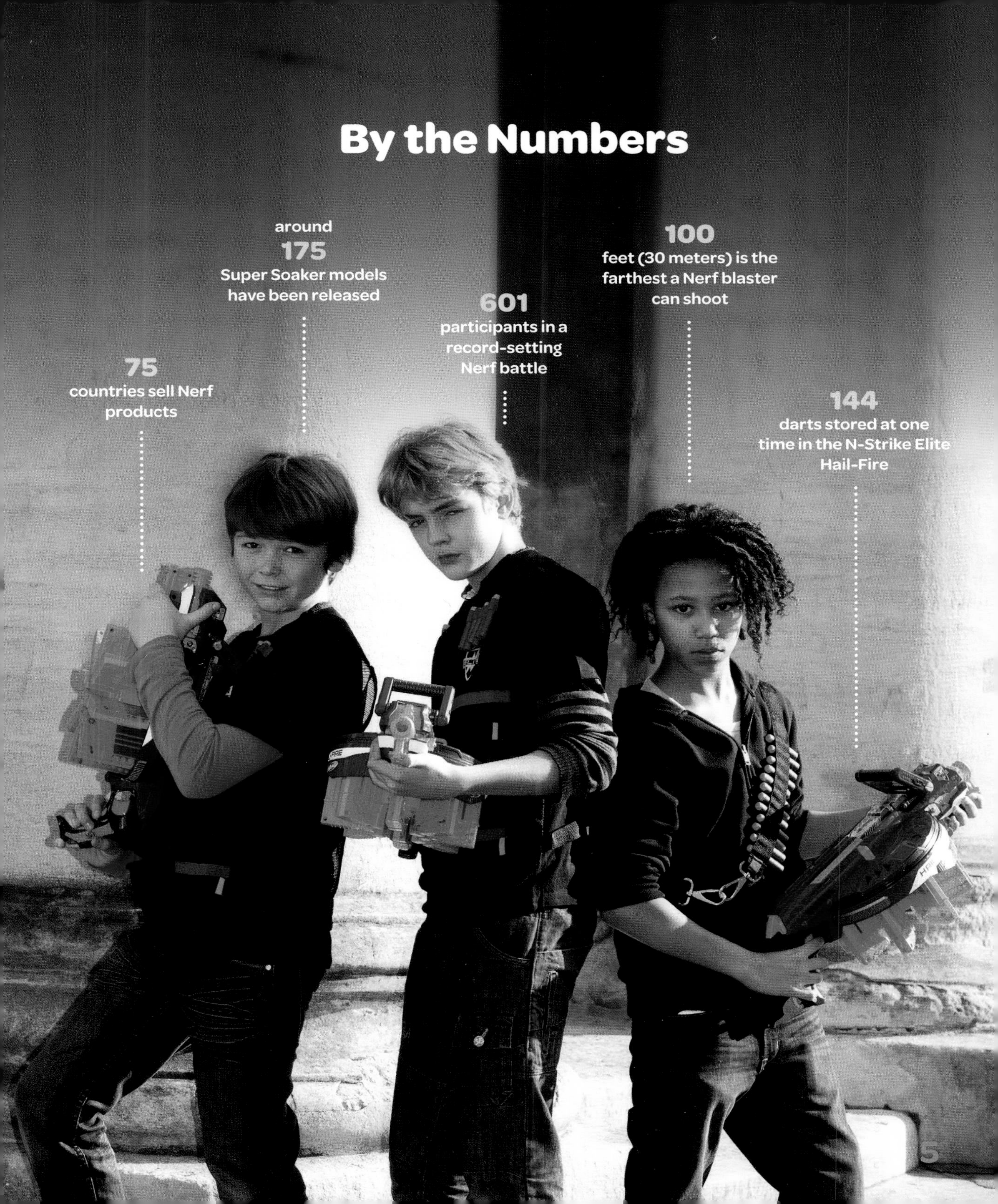

around
175
Super Soaker models
have been released

100
feet (30 meters) is the
farthest a Nerf blaster
can shoot

601
participants in a
record-setting
Nerf battle

75
countries sell Nerf
products

144
darts stored at one
time in the N-Strike Elite
Hail-Fire

How Nerf Began

The Nerf brand started with a ball. A man named Reynolds Guyer, or Reyn, created it in 1969. At that time, Reyn owned a toy company based in St. Paul, Minnesota. He had an idea for a game called "Caveman." To play, people hid fake money under foam rocks. They threw the rocks at each other to prevent stealing. Reyn and his team realized that throwing the foam rocks was the game's best part. They used scissors to cut off the edges of a rock. Now they had an orange, squishy ball. This was the first Nerf ball.

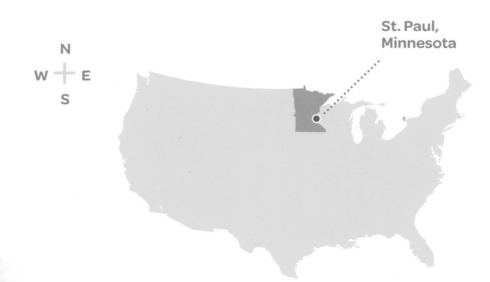

St. Paul, Minnesota

N
W — E
S

Throw it indoors; you can't damage lamps or break windows. You can't hurt babies or old people.

1970s Nerf ball tagline

THE NERF BALL DOES IT ALL!

SOCK SOCCER

HAND TENNIS

NERF BOWL

Nerf BALL

THE WORLD'S FIRST INDOOR BALL

PARKER BROTHERS

Ages 3 and Up

The team presented their toy to a large company called Parker Brothers. In 1970, Nerf balls went on sale for less than a dollar. People loved playing games such as volleyball and basketball inside their homes. By the end of the year, more than 4 million Nerf balls had been sold. The small foam ball was a hit!

The Orange Ornament

The Guyer family still owns the original Nerf ball. Every December, the family hangs it on their Christmas tree as an ornament.

There's only one Nerf

1980s tagline

Fred Cox

A Minnesota Vikings kicker named Fred Cox invented the Nerf football in 1972. A football fan named John Mattox helped give him the idea. Fred still receives money for each Nerf football sold today.

Parker Brothers introduced other fun Nerf products in the 1970s. The Super Nerf ball was one of the first to hit stores. It was larger than the original ball. An indoor basketball game called Nerfoop soon followed. Its backboard could hang on almost any door. In 1972, Nerf began selling foam footballs with thick, rubbery shells. These soared farther and faster than the original Nerf ball. The Nerf football was an instant success. It soon became the best-selling football in the world.

In the 1980s, Parker Brothers expanded the Nerf line. Soon it included indoor golf, ping-pong, hockey, and more. By then, the Nerf name was famous. Parker Brothers began giving the Nerf name to other types of products. People enjoyed writing with Nerf pencils. They played with plastic characters called Nerfuls. They could even chew Nerf chewing gum!

Nerf footballs

Super Nerf ball

Nerfoop

Blasters and More

Over time, several companies helped the Nerf line grow. One was a toy company called Tonka Corporation. It bought Parker Brothers in 1987. Soon, it launched Nerf Blast-A-Ball, the brand's first blaster. Kids shot foam balls out of a plastic tube by pumping the handle. Blast-A-Ball came with two blasters in a box so friends could play together.

In 1991, a larger toy company called Hasbro, Inc. bought the Tonka Corporation. Hasbro quickly expanded the Nerf blaster line. It introduced the Nerf Bow 'n' Arrow and the Slingshot. The Sharp Shooter, Nerf's first dart blaster, arrived in stores in 1992. Dart blasters would soon become the brand's best-known products.

In the early 2000s, the N-Strike blasters first hit store shelves. These yellow and orange weapons fired foam darts with rubber tips. They were Nerf's best blasters yet! N-Strike blasters introduced **tactical rails**. Players could add **barrel extensions**, flip-up **sights**, and other accessories to their blasters. These gave blasters the look of real guns.

Nerf Blasters Over Time

Name	Year Released	Ammunition	Ammo Amount
Blast-A-Ball	1989	balls	1
Ballzooka	1994	balls	15
Big Bad Bow	1998	arrows	3
Maverick REV-6	2005	darts	6
Vulcan EBF-25	2008	darts	25
Vortex Pyragon	2012	discs	40
Strongarm	2013	darts	6
Heartbreaker Bow	2013	darts	6
Rhino-Fire	2014	darts	50
XD Retaliator	2014	darts	12 (with clip)
Barrage Soaker	2014	water	84 fluid ounces (2.5 liters)
Mega RotoFury	2015	whistling darts	10

Maverick REV-6

Strongarm

XD Retaliator

Mega RotoFury

The Nerf design team continues to work hard. Their **innovations** have led to blasters with more power and longer firing ranges. In 2011, Nerf launched a new line of weapons called Vortex. These blasters fire small green, orange, or white discs. Some even glow in the dark! The discs travel farther than most foam darts. The most powerful Vortex blasters can shoot up to 60 feet (18 meters).

A game of **laser** tag is even more thrilling with the Phoenix LTX Tagger. It fires invisible lasers instead of darts. Players aim for their **opponents**' taggers. When they are hit, a red dome on the tagger flashes and beeps.

Bend the rules of battle

2010s Vortex tagline

Nerf Vortex

Combat Creatures Terradrone

Nerf also makes a remote-controlled blaster. Players **activate** the Combat Creatures Terradrone with a handheld remote control. This dart shooter uses six legs to move across all **terrains**. Players destroy opponents with rapid-fire blasting. They can even hit targets 45 feet (14 meters) away!

Zombies Beware!
The Zombie Strike line is one of Nerf's first themed series. Players are encouraged to use its blasters and Super Soakers to take down pretend zombies.

Today, many people think of blasters when they hear the Nerf name. But the brand has not completely strayed from its roots. The N-Sports line features balls, flying discs, and other products. Many N-Sports products have changed how people play with Nerf sports equipment.

One popular product is the Vortex football. Tail fins give these footballs a longer and smoother flight than other Nerf footballs. They even whistle as they soar through the air. The Firevision Sports line was made for playing in the dark. Footballs and basketballs glow with green or red light. But only players wearing special glasses can see them! Playing dodgeball and other games is extra fun with a Nerf Bash ball. Its handholds make it easy to grip and slam.

Nerf Dog

Nerf makes toys especially for dogs. The Nerf Dog line offers a variety of toys for dogs to fetch, tug, and chew.

It's Nerf or Nothin'!

1990s–2010s tagline

Bash ball

203931

15

Expanding the Brand

The Nerf brand has grown to include products for a wider audience. In 1995, Hasbro bought the Super Soaker brand. In time, its water guns were added to Nerf's products. People enjoy **drenching** each other with Super Soakers. They are among the brand's top-selling toys. Some can blast water more than 35 feet (11 meters)!

Rival is a new ball blaster series designed for teenagers and adults. The balls can zip through the air at higher speeds than other Nerf blasters. Some reach 70 miles (113 kilometers) an hour! Face masks give players extra protection. Rival products come in red and blue. This way, team members can identify friends and **foes**.

Rival Zeus MXV-1200 blaster

Super Soaker XP 270

A Super Inventor
The Super Soaker was originally called the Power Drencher. An engineer named Lonnie Johnson invented it in the early 1980s.

The Nerf Rebelle line is especially exciting for girls. Its weapons are stylish in addition to being powerful. The Strongheart Bow is a favorite. It has three regular darts and one dart for secret messages. Another popular item is the Secret Shot Blaster. It looks like a purse. But watch out! It is actually a powerful dart blaster with a long range.

Nerf Wars

Nerf wars happen in backyards, parks, or anywhere with space to move and hide. Some kids use blasters to add an extra level of excitement to classic games like Capture the Flag. Others play new games such as Humans vs. Zombies. Some people even join Nerf leagues. These are often fought in indoor areas that look like cities or military zones. Darts for these wars have Velcro tips. They stick to special vests worn by players. A player tagged by a dart is out. After players divide into teams, blaster battles begin!

In 2014, Nerf revealed it was working on new technology. The Tek Strike line of accessories will use wireless technology to keep track of players' hits and ammo. For even more action, players will be able to download a Tek Strike **app**. It allows them to use mobile devices to unlock weapons and track teams. Indoors or outdoors, Nerf keeps battles safe, fun, and exciting!

Nerf Timeline

1969
Reyn Guyer invents the
Nerf ball

1972
The basketball game
Nerfoop is introduced

1972
The Nerf football
is launched

1970
The first Nerf balls
are sold in stores

1983
The Nerf baseball
is introduced

1989
Blast-A-Ball debuts

1992
The Sharp Shooter
is released

1991
Hasbro, Inc. begins
selling Nerf products

1991
Bow 'n' Arrow
is introduced

2003
The N-Strike
line begins

2011
Nerf wins Boy Toy of the
Year and Outdoor Toy of
the Year at the American
International Toy Fair

2010
The Super Soaker series
becomes part of the
Nerf line

2012
The Firevision Sports
line is introduced

2015
The Rival series
begins

2012
The N-Strike Elite
line is released

2009
The first Nerf Dart
Tag League World
Championship is held

2013
The Zombie Strike
line hits stores

2014
The Combat Creatures
Terradrone is introduced

Glossary

accessories—things added to something else to make it more useful or attractive

activate—start up

ammunition—material fired from weapons

app—a small, specialized program downloaded onto smartphones and other mobile devices

barrel extensions—parts added to the ends of guns to improve their performance

brand—a category of products all made by the same company

clips—devices inserted into guns that store rounds of ammunition

drenching—soaking with water

foes—enemies

headquarters—a company's main office

innovations—new methods, products, or ideas

laser—a device that produces a sharp, narrow beam of light

opponents—people to compete against

sights—parts added to guns to help people aim or find the direction of an object

tactical rails—brackets on weapons that provide places to add accessories and attachments

terrains—types of land

To Learn More

AT THE LIBRARY

Green, Sara. *Lego*. Minneapolis, Minn.: Bellwether Media, 2015.

Marunas, Nathaniel. *The Ultimate Nerf Blaster Book*. Brooklyn, N.Y.: Pow!, 2013.

Wulffson, Don. *Toys!: Amazing Stories Behind Some Great Inventions*. New York, N.Y.: Square Fish, 2014.

ON THE WEB

Learning more about Nerf is as easy as 1, 2, 3.

1. Go to www.factsurfer.com.

2. Enter "Nerf" into the search box.

3. Click the "Surf" button and you will see a list of related web sites.

With factsurfer.com, finding more information is just a click away.

Index